Barack Obama

Caroline Crosson Gilpin

NATIONAL
GEOGRAPHIC

Washington, D.C.

For the children of the Edward Williams Elementary
School, Mount Vernon, New York —C.C.G.

The publisher and author gratefully acknowledge the expert review
of this book by David Coleman, associate professor, Presidential Recordings Program,
Miller Center, University of Virginia.

Paperback ISBN: 978-1-4263-1759-0
Reinforced Library Binding ISBN: 978-1-4263-1760-6

Book design by YAY! Design

Photo Credits

CO: Corbis; GI: Getty Images; SS: Shutterstock
Cover, Kwaku Alston/CO Outline; (background), DanielW/SS; 1, Doug Mills/Pool/10137457A/CO; 2 (UP), Mlly Riley/Pool/CO; 2 (LO),
Nathan Bilow/AP Images; 4–5, Chuck Kennedy/Poo/AP Images; 5 (INSET), Pete Souza/Library of Congress Prints & Photographs Division; 6, Obama Presidential Campaign/AP Images; 7, Obama Presidential Campaign/AP Images; 9 (LE), Stock Connection/Super-
Stock ; 9 (RT), Laura S. L. Kong/GI; 10, Obama For America/Handout/Reuters; 11, American Stock Archive/Archive Photos Creative/GI;
12, Saul Loeb/AFP/GettyImages; 13 (UP), STR/Reuters/CO; 13 (CTR), Joe Wrinn/Harvard University/Handout/Brooks Kraft/CO; 13 (LO),
spirit of america/SS; 14, Michael Ward/GI; 15, Obama Presidential Campaign/AP Images; 16, Peter Macdiarmid/GI; 17, Joe Wrinn/
Harvard University/Handout/CO; 18, Obama for America/AP Images; 19, Polaris; 20, Mike Fanous/Gamma-Rapho via GI; 21, Scott
Olson/GI; 23, Brooks Kraft/CO; 24-25, Steve Collender/SS; 24 (UPLE), Jewel Samad/AFP/GI/Newscom; 24 (CTR), Chip Somodevilla/GI;
24 (LO), White House Photo/Alamy; 24 (UPRT), Thomas Mukoya/Reuters; 25 (UPLE), spirit of america/SS; 25 (UPRT), Nigel Pavitt/JAI/
CO; 25 (CTR LE), SSPL/GI; 25 (CTR RT), Dirck Halstead/Liaison/GI; 25 (LOLE), Moneta Sleet, Jr./Ebony Collection/AP Images; 25 (LORT),
General Photographic Agency/GI; 26-27, poofy/SS; 27 (UPLE), Ahmad Al-Rubaye/AFP/GI; 27 (UPRT), John Moore/GI; 27 (LO), Andrew
Harrer/Bloomberg via GI; 28, David Goldman/AP Images; 29, Jewel Samad/AFP/GI; 30 (UP), Pete Souza/Library of Congress Prints &
Photographs Division; 30 (CTR), Stock Connection/SuperStock ; 30 (LO), Obama Presidential Campaign/AP Images; 31 (UP), White
House Photo/Alamy; 31 (CTR RT), Mike Fanous/Gamma-Rapho via GI; 31 (CTR LE), Joe Wrinn/Harvard University/Handout/CO; 31 (LO),
Orhan Cam/SS; 32 (UPLE), Ron Chapple/Taxi/GI ; 32 (UPRT), Angela Weiss/GI; 32 (CTR LE), Rob Marmion/SS; 32 (CTR RT), Russell Lee/
Library of Congress Prints & Photographs Division; 32 (LOLE), Chip Somodevilla/GI; 32 (LORT), Larry Downing/AFP/GI; top border
(throughout), John T Takai/SS; vocabulary boxes, Mike McDonald/SS

National Geographic supports K–12 educators with ELA Common Core Resources.
Visit natgeoed.org/commoncore for more information.

Printed in the United States of America
14/WOR/1

Table of Contents

Meet Barack Obama!

It was cold on January 20, 2009. Barack Hussein Obama stood in front of the waiting crowd.

He raised his hand and swore to protect the country. The crowd cheered for America's first African-American president.

A Hawaiian Beginning

Barack Obama was born in 1961 in Hawaii, U.S.A. His mother was from Kansas, U.S.A. His father was from Kenya, Africa. They met as college students at the University of Hawaii.

That's a Fact! His favorite children's book is *Where the Wild Things Are.*

Obama never really knew his father. When he was just two years old, his father moved away. When Obama was six, his mother remarried and had another child. The family moved across the Pacific Ocean to Indonesia. Obama spent lots of time with his stepfather. He taught Obama to box.

Barack Obama with his mother and half-sister, Maya, and his Indonesian stepfather, Lolo Soetoro.

Childhood

After four years, his mother wanted a better education for her children. She sent Obama back to Hawaii to stay with his grandparents. There, he attended the Punahou School.

Obama played on the basketball team and did well in his classes.

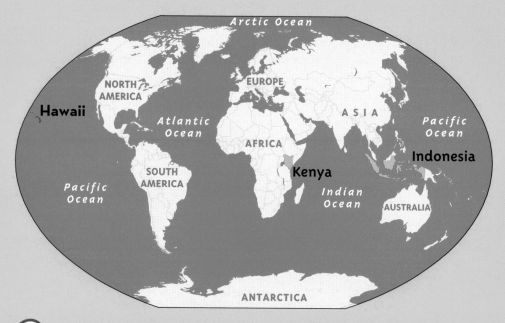

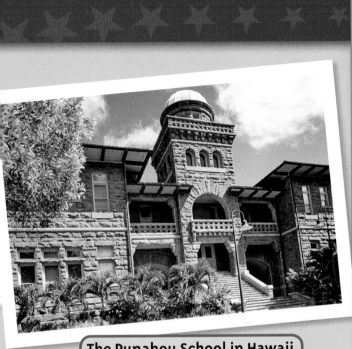

The Punahou School in Hawaii

Hawaii had many multiracial (MULL-tee RAY-shul) families, but few African Americans. Obama was one of only three black students at his school. He started to notice racism there.

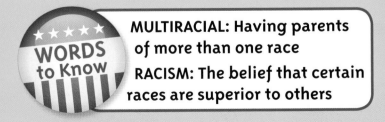

WORDS to Know

MULTIRACIAL: Having parents of more than one race

RACISM: The belief that certain races are superior to others

Obama felt different from other students and wished his father was there to teach him about his African family.

When Obama was ten, his father came to visit him from Kenya. Obama was excited to spend a whole month with his dad.

Obama's father lived in Nairobi, Kenya.

Obama's father visited Punahou School. He spoke to the class about Kenya. Obama was sad when he left. It was the last time he ever saw his father.

That's a Fact! Obama was called "Barry" before he went to college. Then he began using his full name, Barack.

Obama's Cool "Firsts"

You already know Barack Obama is the first African–American president. But do you know these other "firsts"?

Barack Obama is the first president to own and use a smartphone.

Obama on a call during his 2012 presidential campaign

Barack Obama is the first U.S. president to receive the Nobel Peace Prize during his first year as president.

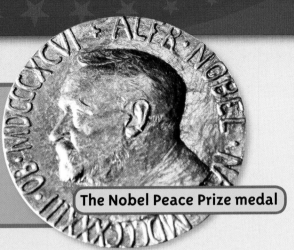

The Nobel Peace Prize medal

Obama's class photo while he was president of the *Harvard Law Review*

Barack Obama is the first African-American president of the *Harvard Law Review*. The *Law Review* is a respected magazine published by students at Harvard Law School.

Barack Obama is the first president from Hawaii. His mother and grandparents moved there in 1960.

State flag of Hawaii

Community and College

Obama lived in New York City, New York, during college. He saw how racism was affecting the lives of poor black Americans. Many had no money. Others had no jobs. This bothered Obama. He wanted to help people improve their lives.

A homeless person in New York City in 1983

Obama signing up voters

Obama graduated from college
and moved to Chicago, Illinois.
He became a community organizer.
He helped poor people find homes
they could
afford and
register to vote.

WORDS to Know

COMMUNITY ORGANIZER: A leader who works to improve neighborhoods

Law School and Politics

In 1982, Obama's father died. Obama traveled to Kenya and met all his African relatives.

Obama with his African relatives

That's a Fact! Obama is six feet one inch tall.

Obama at Harvard Law School in 1990

His father had been a leader there. That made Obama want to be a leader himself. How could he start? Obama thought he should become a lawyer. He applied to Harvard University, where his father had attended. He studied hard and graduated with high honors.

Obama teaching a class at the University of Chicago

Now Obama was ready to use his education. He wanted to help others be treated fairly. He moved back to Chicago to work as a civil rights lawyer. He also taught law classes to college students.

Obama dreamed of doing important things. He decided to run for the Illinois State Senate. He won the election in 1996. In 2004, he won the election for an even bigger job—U.S. senator.

Barack and Michelle Obama were married in Chicago in 1992.

WORDS to Know

CIVIL RIGHTS LAWYER: A lawyer who makes sure people receive fair and equal treatment

SENATOR: One kind of elected member of the United States government

Road to the Presidency

In 2004, Barack Obama was asked to give the main speech at the Democratic National Convention. This was an important event. He wrote the speech himself and became famous for it. His speech gave people hope for the future.

In His Own Words

"There is not a Black America and White America and Latino America and Asian America—there's the United States of America."

People wanted the government to change. Obama thought he could do that. So he decided to run for president. His campaign (kam–PANE) slogans were "Yes We Can" and "Change We Can Believe In."

How could Obama win? He was just 47 years old, very young to be president. His campaign did not have a lot of money, and there had never been a black president before.

Obama didn't let this stop him. He used the Internet to organize volunteers and to raise money.

On Election Day in November, 2008, Barack Obama won! He became the first African-American president. The White House was Obama's new home.

Barack, Sasha, Malia, and Michelle Obama on Election Night 2008

8 Cool Facts

1

Obama has eight half brothers and sisters, from his mother's and father's other marriages.

2

Obama is left-handed.

3

Obama has two "first dogs," Bo and Sunny.

4

Obama can speak Spanish.

5

The name Barack means "one who is blessed" in Swahili.

6

Obama likes to play Scrabble.

7

Obama owns a red pair of boxing gloves once owned by Muhammad Ali.

8

Obama's heroes are Martin Luther King, Jr., and Mahatma Gandhi.

The Nation's Leader

In his first term as president, Obama had many goals. He wanted to bring home U.S. soldiers who were fighting overseas. He wanted more people to have health care. And he wanted more Americans to be able to find jobs.

WORDS to Know

TERM: A fixed or limited period of time

U.S. soldiers in Iraq

A job fair in New York City

President Obama addresses Congress.

1990

Becomes first African American to be elected as president of *Harvard Law Review*

1991

Graduates from law school, becomes civil rights lawyer in Chicago, teaches law at the University of Chicago

1992

Marries Michelle Robinson on October 18

27

Obama worked hard to meet his goals. But the problems Americans face are very hard to fix. After four years, Obama wanted more time to make changes. In 2012, he ran for a second term and won!

1996
Wins election to the Illinois Senate

2004
Delivers main speech at Democratic National Convention; elected U.S. senator in November

2007
Announces he will run for president of the United States

28

A new president will take over in 2017. But for now, there is still much to do.

In His Own Words

"The best way to not feel hopeless is to get up and do something. Don't wait for good things to happen to you. If you go out and make some good things happen, you will fill the world with hope, you will fill yourself with hope."

2008
Elected 44th president of the United States

2009
Wins Nobel Peace Prize

2012
Wins second term as U.S. president in November

Be a Quiz Whiz!

See how many questions you can get right! Answers are at the bottom of page 31.

1

Barack Obama is the _____ president of the United States.
A. 30th
B. 44th
C. 12th
D. 40th

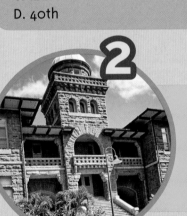

2

Obama graduated from Punahou High School. Which state is it in?
A. Indonesia
B. Hawaii
C. California
D. New York

3

Before becoming president, Obama worked as a _____.
A. Community organizer
B. Law professor
C. U.S. senator
D. All of the above

What are the two first dogs' names?
A. Martha and Murphy
B. Bode and Maggie
C. Bo and Sunny
D. Splash and Roscoe

Obama first became famous in politics when he _____.
A. Moved to Chicago
B. Gave an important speech
C. Got married
D. Traveled to Kenya

While a law student, Obama was selected to be the first African-American president of the *Harvard Law Review*.
A. True
B. False

What year was Obama elected to be a U.S. senator?
A. 1992
B. 1996
C. 2004
D. 2012

CIVIL RIGHTS LAWYER: A lawyer who makes sure people receive fair and equal treatment

COMMUNITY ORGANIZER: A leader who works to improve neighborhoods

MULTIRACIAL: Having parents of more than one race

RACISM: The belief that certain races are superior to others

SENATOR: One kind of elected member of the United States government

TERM: A fixed or limited period of time